Front Cover: A view from Punch Bowl Lane bri
in September 1960, as a BR class 2MT 2-6-2T leaves Chesham with the Ashbury [illegible]
of about 1900 vintage. In the background the electrification work is almost complete with the new bay platform in place. (*T. A. Murphy/Colour-Rail BRM1157*)

Inside Front Cover, top: The evocative picture that met the passengers entering Chesham Station in the days of steam. On a warm summer's day in June 1957 ex-GC class C13 no.67420 hisses faintly at the front of the teak Ashbury coaches which form the 'Shuttle' - and is there honey still for tea?. (*Colour-Rail*)

Inside Front Cover, bottom: The branch has always been a favourite destination for special trains and here, in June 1956, the 'John Milton' waits at Chesham to leave for Baker Street. LT no.48, which was ex-MET E class no.81, with it's matching Dreadnought coaches recreates a common scene of 30 years earlier.
(*L V Reason/Colour-Rail LT134*)

Inside Rear Cover, top: Specials have continued after electrification of the branch. On 24th August 1969 a set of veteran 1935 red 'Q' stock made a LT rail tour to Chesham to mark the Centenary of the District Line. (*Rodney Flanagan*)

Inside Rear Cover, bottom: In the dawn light at Chesham in July 1962 with a class 115 DMU being prepared to form the 05.58 to Marylebone. The train has delivered papers along the MET and is a last reminder that this was once the Metropolitan & Great Central Joint Committee line. (*G H Hunt/Colour-Rail LT191*)

Back Cover, top: In the foreground are the watercress beds near the bridge at Waterside as the sun slowly rises over the Chess Valley on the morning of 25th June 1960. Meanwhile commuters head for London on the 08.05 'through' train to Liverpool Street headed by no.76042, a BR 4MT 2-6-0. (*Colour-Rail*)

Back Cover, bottom: The 35 years old LT aluminium A60 stock were refurbished by ABB and this picture in May 1996 at Chalfont & Latimer shows a BR type 37 diesel hauling such a set to their Derby works for the retrofit. A match wagon is marshalled between the loco and LT stock in order to accommodate the different couplings. (*Ron Potter*)

PREFACE

I suspect that many might wonder why the Chesham branch of the erstwhile Metropolitan Railway deserves one book let alone two! However, my earlier book 'Chesham Shuttle' was well received and seemed to strike a chord with local people who were interested in the protracted origins of the line, its impact on the development of the Chilterns and survival against considerable odds. Equally, the railway fraternity seemed attracted by the story of the changing ownership and surprising variety of motive power. As a result I received many pleasant letters from all over the U.K. containing reminiscences of the MET and often enclosing old photographs or other memorabilia. In addition, my earlier contacts continued to produce more information and I have collected a selection giving a pictorial perspective on a much-loved railway byway. These are roughly in chronological order and I have included more relating to the mainline through Chalfont & Latimer in order to illustrate the wide range of connecting services that were once available – albeit for those with time to kill to reach their destinations to the north.

It is hoped that the picture of the Metropolitan Railway relief map and the reproduction in the middle pages of the little-known London Transport souvenir, marking the completion of the electrification programme in 1961, will provide enough background information to make this booklet self-sufficient.

The origins of photographs are indicted in most captions and permission for their use has been sought wherever possible. In particular I am most grateful to Ray East who loaned several prints from his collection and also to Ron White who, as 'Colour-Rail', kindly provided most of the colour illustrations together with some rare B/W shots from his own archive. My special thanks are also due to Frank Bunker, Jean Catherine, Robert Clark, Fred Cooper, Tony Geary, John Gercken, Susan Gradidge, Chris Hawkins, Michael Hance, Julian Hunt, Ken Palmer, Jean Podbury, Ron Potter, Maurice Sawyer, Colin Seabright, Tony Weedon and Phyllis Woodstock for their contributions, plus very many others. The assistance provided by the staffs at the London Transport Museum, Locomotive Club of Great Britain, Buckinghamshire Record Office, Aylesbury Reference Library, Chesham Reference Library, 'Bucks Examiner' and the National Monuments Record is also much appreciated. Nevertheless I remain responsible for any errors that do appear.

Clive Foxell

Autumn 1998, Chesham

The Metropolitan Railway displayed this attractive relief map at Baker Street Station and the terrain clearly shows the barrier of the Chiltern Hills, which proved such a problem for the railway pioneers who wished to construct lines to the northwest of London. In between the GWR to the west and the L&BR (LNWR) to the north-west the area between of the Chiltern Hundreds was the scene of many competing proposals for new railways, but nothing came of these and this part of Buckinghamshire remained without a railway for over 50 years. But then salvation came from a surprising direction, when that archetypal Victorian entrepreneur and megalomaniac, Sir Edward Watkin, became Chairman of the struggling Metropolitan Railway and incorporated it into his grandiose vision for a rail-link between Manchester and Paris.

By 1880 the revitalised MET had reached Harrow and Watkin started to build the 'Extension' on to the prosperous town of Chesham in the expectation of connecting with the LNWR at Tring. Unfortunately he had to take-up another of the options he had in reserve and acquired the railway interests of the Duke of Buckingham, enabling the MET to divert north from Chalfont Road to Verney Junction where he hoped to link-up with his newly-named Great Central Railway coming from the north. (*LT Museum*)

By the mid - 19th century the town of Chesham had grown to population of over 6,000 people but for over 50 years the only access to a railway was by horse-drawn cart or coach. Here the LNWR coach with passengers for Berkhamsted Station prepares to leave Chesham Broadway and tackle the stiff climb up Nashleigh Hill. (*Ray East*)

Construction of the MET line began in 1887. The railway had to drop down along the side of the Chess Valley at 1 in 66, which involved major embankments and cuttings through the chalk. This picture shows the work at Millfields where sidings were laid to extract gravel for use elsewhere, thus creating more of the famed watercress beds. (*Ray East*)

The ‘navvies’ who built the first railways lived rough and were noted for their rowdy behaviour. But by this time they had become more domesticated and the local people even gave them all a Christmas party in 1888. This motley group includes the foreman wearing his traditional tall hat, with his men, plus the young boy to get the tea. (*Frank Bunker*)

Watkin planned to extend the line to Tring but the Chesham terminus was to be sited on The Moor, an inconvenient distance from the town. As a result the local people subscribed to a fund to enable the railway station to be built near the High Street. This view shows the line curving round on the left to cross the River Chess and Waterside. (*Frank Bunker*)

The new railway bridge over the River Chess with Waterside in the background and the Cottage Hospital on the right up the hill. In those days Dell Spring added to the flow of water at this point to help power the remaining mills on the river but in building the bridge the MET had to agree "not to intercept the flow of water or disturb the fish"! (*Ray East*)

The scene in Chesham High Street in the early 1880's looking towards Market Square. When the MET built the station in 1888 it created access to the High Street by demolishing the two houses on the left, beyond the Misses Catling's shop with the awning that protected their display of millinery in the windows from the sun. (*Frank Bunker*)

Most goods traffic for the railway at Chesham flowed through the gates in Whitehill. However, the new Station Road (shown here about 1894 and complete with chickens) not only gave direct access for passengers to the Station and livestock to the pens, but also established The Broadway as the centre of the town. (*Colin Seabright*)

Ploughing the field behind the Chesham Brewery, where the main goods yard was to be laid-out, and now the site of Waitrose car park. This brewery was to provide not only much business for the railway in terms of coal & hops coming-in and beer going-out, but also in the aroma that permeated the area and samples for the deliverymen! (*Ray East*)

The main celebration for arrival of the railway was held on the 18th May 1889 marking the 'Inspection by the Directors' and this is the scene at Chesham Station after the quiet public opening of the line on 8th July. Watkin abandoned his plan to extend the line through the goods yard to Tring, however BR retained some of the relevant land till 1996. (*Ray East*)

Instead the MET diverted north from Chalfont Road in 1892 – here with a new Aylesbury bound train arriving - and Chesham became a branch. Initially the carriages were brought from Chesham and attached to the rear of the mainline trains but this soon changed to the well-known 'Shuttle' service, which (hopefully) made the connection. (*Colin Seabright*)

Nevertheless, the traditional pattern of operation was soon established with the provision of 'through' trains for Chesham in the morning and evening for workers in the City. Here, with such a train at the original Harrow on the Hill station on 31.2.1902, is one of the early classic MET class A 4-4-0 tank engines no.17, named "Ixion". (*Ken Nunn/ LCGB*)

Watkin encouraged the MS&LR to extend south to a new terminus at Marylebone and to become the GCR. This route involved using the MET Extension from 1899, but the testing gradients, congestion and disputes over profit sharing led to dissatisfaction within the GCR. Here in 1907 the Royal Train, headed by a new Robinson 4-4-2 no.365, is passing the open fields after Chalfont Road. King Edward V11 was bound for Wendover and a rendezvous at Lord Alfred Rothschild's Halton House. (*Ray East/R..Hardy*)

When Watkin became ill his autocratic rule weakened and his empire began to disintegrate. In 1906 this was resolved by forming a Metropolitan & Great Central Joint Committee to own the Extension lines. This picture shows the interior of Chesham booking office around 1908 with James Woodward, assisted by 'Tug' Wilson, surrounded by the traditional array of Edmonson card tickets and date stamp. (*Jean Podbury*)

A consequence of the joint operation was that the more luxurious GCR trains now ran from Chesham to Marylebone. Here their class 9N 4-6-2T no.23 waits to leave around 1912, providing a backdrop for the branch permanent way gang. In practice the MET maintained the track as far as Great Missenden and the GCR to the north. (*Ray East*)

In 1908 Robert Selbie took control of the MET rationalised the rambling inheritance from Watkin under the banner of MetroLand. However, some of the by-now elderly class A tank engines still operated without proper cabs at the outbreak of the First War, and here no.27 rests beside the very basic coaling stage at Chesham station. (*LT Museum*)

As part of the MET drive to promote a positive image two Pullman cars were introduced to provide refreshments on peak trains. This picture shows the Chesham train with 'Mayflower' at Baker Street, but the service was withdrawn soon after the out-break of war in 1939. However, the idea resurfaced in 1951, but was rejected "as we are not the right people to do stunts of this nature - not even the Metropolitan line". (*LT Museum*)

This picture, and the one opposite, were taken from roughly the same position above the 'Baulks' and provide a panorama of Chesham Station from the north. The date of this part is about 1920 and shows the station buildings with the roofed top of the water tower to where stationmen sometimes retreated in the summer in order to have a rest. (*Ray East*)

LOCAL DATA OF RESIDENTIAL DISTRICTS IN METRO-LAND.

Station.	Trains (each way) daily.	Journey time to or from Baker St.	Local Rates (in the £).	Gas per 1000 feet (*a*): per th'm (*b*).	Charge for Water.	Electric Light (per unit).	Altitude above sea level.	Subsoil.
Willesden Green	282	8 mts.	11/6	3/7 (*a*)	6½% rate val.	4d.	180 ft.	Clay
Neasden	222	12 ,,	9/4	3/7 (*a*)	5¾% ,,	4d.	127 ft.	Gravel and clay
Wembley Park	287	11 ,,	9/6	3/10 (*a*)	7% ,,	4d.	234 ft.	Clay
Preston Road	119	13 ,,	9/6	3/10 (*a*)	7% ,,	4d.	162 ft.	,,
Northwick Park & Kenton ..	131	14 ,,	9/6	3/10 (*a*)	7% ,,	4d.	175 ft.	,,
Harrow-on-the-Hill	193	15 ,,	7/8	3/9 (*a*)	6-8.4% ,,	5d.	400 ft.	,,
West Harrow	77	19 ,,	8/6	3/9 (*a*)	6-8.4% ,,	4½d.	196 ft.	,,
Rayners Lane (for Harrow Garden Village)	75	21 ,,	8/4	1/- (*b*)	6½% ,,	6½d.	175 ft.	Loamy clay
Eastcote	45	23 ,,	10/2	1/- (*b*)	5½-7% plus 20%	6½d.	196 ft.	,,
Ruislip	49	25 ,,	10/2	1/- (*b*)	5½-7% plus 20%	6½d.	168 ft.	Gravel and clay
Ickenham	44	28 ,,	11/10	1/- (*b*)	5% rate val.	6d.	207 ft.	,, ,,
Hillingdon	45	30 ,,	11/10	1/- (*b*)	5% ,,	6d.	117 ft.	,, ,,
Uxbridge	49	30 ,,	12/-	1/- (*b*)	1/4 in £ rate val.	6d.	200 ft.	,, ,,
North Harrow	68	19 ,,	8/5½	1/- (*b*)	6-8.4% ,,	6½d.	175 ft.	Clay
Pinner..	68	21 ,,	9/1	5/- (*a*)	6-8.4% ,,	6½d.	163-230 ft.	,,
Northwood	72	23 ,,	10/2	1/- (*b*)	5½-7% plus 20%	6½d.	200-450 ft.	Gravel and clay
Moor Park & Sandy Lodge ..	54	30 ,,	11/-	1/0½ (*b*)	5% gross val.	8d.	380 ft.	Gravel and chalk
Croxley Green	45	32 ,,	10/8	1/0½ (*b*)	5% ,,	8d.	350 ft.	,, ,,
Watford	47	34 ,,	11/10	9¼ (*b*)	1/- in £ ,,	3d.	150-350 ft.	,, ,,
Rickmansworth	46	27 ,,	11/-	1/0½ (*b*)	5% gross val.	8d.	150-270 ft.	,, ,,
Chorley Wood & Chenies ..	39	34 ,,	10/4	13.9d. (*b*)	5% rate val.	8d.	368 ft.	,, ,,
Chalfont & Latimer	40	38 ,,	10/6	1/- (*b*)	5⅔% ,,	7d.	410 ft.	,, ,,
Chesham	26	48 ,,	11/6	11d. (*b*)	10d. in £ per yr.	7d.	330-526 ft.	,, ,,
Amersham & Chesham Bois ..	32	40 ,,	10/2	1/- (*b*)	7½% rate val.	7d.	300-540 ft.	,, ,,
Great Missenden	28	49 ,,	10/-	1/- (*b*)	5⅔% ,,	7d.	400-600 ft.	,, ,,
Wendover	26	58 ,,	10/-	1/6 (*b*)	7½% gross val.	8d.	450-900 ft.	,, ,,
Aylesbury	27	73 ,,	13/-	1/4 (*b*)	6½% rate val.	8d.	275 ft.	Clay & friable rock

The MET annually published a booklet extolling the attractions of MetroLand, including a table, such as this one from the 1932 edition, which presented information to guide the prospective commuter on the relative costs of living along the Extension.

The companion to the picture on the left, taken around 1906, and showing the extensive goods yard with cattle pens and tree trunks awaiting delivery. In the foreground on the left the 'Shuttle' waits with its primitive 8-wheel rigid coaches that opened the service and were the cause of much passenger discomfort. (*Bucks County Records & Local Studies*)

In response to the better coaches of the GCR the old 8-wheel rigid MET coaches were replaced by 'Dreadnought's' as shown here at Chalfont, headed by no.81 one of the elegant E class 0-4-4 tank engines. The branch was operated by 'tablet' and sadly a signalman, Mr Saint, was killed as he stepped back into the path of an express. (*C Foxell*)

'Dreadnought' stock were already employed on the mainline MET trains and no.110, one of the H class 4-4-4T's, leaves Chalfont & Latimer with the 5.04pm ex-Chesham for Baker Street on 10.6.1933. The leading coach carries the pick-up gear on the front bogie for use on the electrified section after Rickmansworth. (*Ken Nunn Collection/LCGB*)

At Chalfont & Latimer there were delays due to the need for the engine to take the 'Shuttle' coaches out of the bay platform in order to do a 'gravity' shunt and couple to the other end for the return journey. But, as with this 'Shuttle' hauled by MET 1 on 17.6.1933, often wagons had to be manoeuvred as well. (*Ken Nunn Collection/LCGB*)

After marshalling the wagons into the right order they were collected by the daily pick-up goods. The powerful K class 2-6-4T's were introduced to cope with the growing freight traffic and above MET 116 on the ex-8.10 am Verney Junction has left Chalfont on 10.6.1933 for Harrow goods depot. (*Ken Nunn Collection/LCGB*)

Something was usually happening in Chesham yard to provide a ready distraction for the pupils of Whitehill School that overlooked the scene. The larger MET tanks were very tall and had distinctive front steps facing forwards, here clearly shown on H Class no.105 as it waits beside the Brewery in 1935. (*Clive Foxell Collection*)

A group of boys who might have been the prototypes for Richmal Compton's 'Just William' gang pose in awe on the down platform at Chalfont & Latimer. From the lack of the shelter and awning the date would seem to be around 1930 and interestingly, in the background, the weekly changeover of the 'Shuttle' is taking place. (*NMR*)

Bob Geary, who helped to build the branch, stayed on with the MET as a member of the permanent way gang who walked the line each day, maintaining it in tiptop condition and cutting back the undergrowth. Many of his relations were railwaymen and here he is standing in front of the prize-winning gardens at Chesham around 1930. (*Maurice Sawyer*)

Watkin's expectation of tapping a significant amount of freight business at Chesham was justified. This is shown indirectly by the number of staff shown here from the goods office and there would be others involved in collection and delivery. Ada Long, on the right, was the first woman to work there in 1915 and she left to marry George Weedon, next to her, in 1925. She celebrated her 100th birthday in 1997. (*Family of Ada Weedon*)

By 1927 some 5,000 tons per month of freight were passing through Chesham. Domestic coal suppliers often had their own 'private owner' wagons to bring fuel from the mines and this example was built for the local merchant A H Rance, which must have looked a magnificent sight in dark red with white lining shaded in black. (*Clive Foxell Collection*)

Although in theory the Met & GC Jt Cttee operated the freight, in practice it was run by the MET. Wood products were steady trade at Chesham Stn but a number of engineering businesses were established and here a horse-drawn wagon is collecting some metalwork. Note the crude boiler on the right and the wood to stop the horse moving on. (*Ray East*)

Passenger trains collected milk churns daily and the MET built special ventilated vans, such as this, for the traffic to London. Racing pigeons also created a steady trade and a guard, who often had to release them from Woodford for the flight back to Chesham, said that one bird was so used to the trip that it returned on the roof of the train! (*Clive Foxell*)

Bulk shipments of milk were also collected at depots such as Dorrington in Shropshire and here former GCR 4-4-2 now an LNER class C4 no.6085 - known as a 'Jersey Lily' after the elegant singer Lily Langtry - returns past the Chesham Branch in 1934 on a down train of a few empty tank wagons from Marylebone. (C R L Coles)

Very large items were also handled by the railway and this shows the final step in the special delivery in October 1936 of a 72 ft long steel girder weighing 15 tons in Chesham, where it was to support the 'circle' of the new Embassy Cinema. The clock on the old Town Hall indicates that it is 8 minutes past midnight. (*Clive Foxell Collection*)

National Benzole established an oil depot at Chalfont & Latimer and soon afterwards, in 1933, a rake of their smart silver-painted tank wagons is at rest at the station-end of the yard. In the foreground is one of the MET brake vans with the distinctive guard's hand brake mounted on the outside of the veranda. (*H. C. Casserley*)

All stock suffered from lack of maintenance during the war and here some similar oil tanker wagons, now dirty and rusty, are seen having been shunted in a rather energetic manner at the oil depot in Chalfont & Latimer. The date of the incident is around 1961 and the terminal was closed completely in 1967. (*Jean Catherine*)

Another large load in Chesham goods yard. At the top of the picture the hook of the 8-ton crane has been removed after lifting a new steam boiler for Beechwood Brushes onto a trailer, now to be hauled by the traction engine to Higham Road. (*Ray East*)

Ernie Woodstock started working for the Met & GC Jt. Ctte. in the goods yard at the age of 14 years in 1927 and this picture shows him in the 1930's driving one of the ubiquitous Scammell 3-wheel tractors. These vehicles with their trailers were highly manoeuvrable vehicles but were fairly basic as illustrated by the cab and the horn. (*Phyllis Woodstock*)

With the death of Selbie there was a certain inevitability in the acquisition of the MET by London Transport in 1932. They disliked the steam services that they inherited on the Extension and sought to replace them. The first experiment was with an AEC-built railcar loaned by the GWR for an unsuccessful trial on the Chesham Branch in March 1936.

The next step by LT in 1937 was to pass most of their ex-MET steam locomotive stock over to the LNER and now a mixture of MET and LNER engines were seen on the branch. Here a 4-6-2 tank class A5 no.5449 waits in Chesham Station next to an ex- GC coach with its distinctive toothed anti-collision device over the buffers.

Under the Government's "New Works Programme" in the late 1930's, LT started planning to electrify the 'Extension'. Preliminary civil engineering works began and this picture shows one of the many mock-ups of proposed rolling stock with open layout coaches and air-operated doors, but all work was suspended at the outbreak of war. (*LT*)

In 1941 the 'Shuttle' was simplified by changing to "auto-working" thereby avoiding the need for the engine to run-round the coaches at either end of the trip. The motive power was provided by some LNER C13 4-4-2T's of 1903 and LT matched these with their own Ashbury coaches that had already seen 42 years service in many guises. (*H C Casserley*)

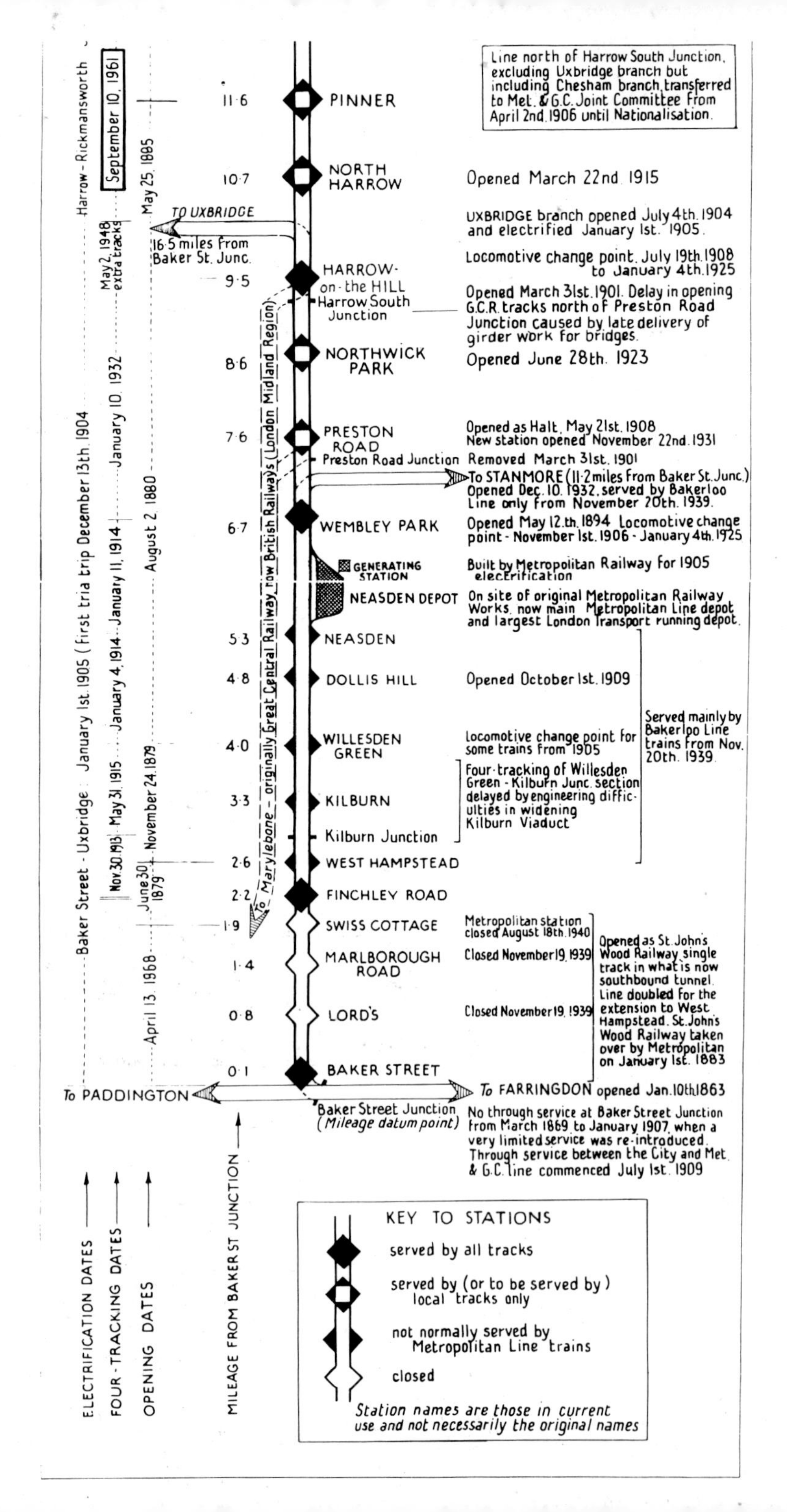
Line north of Harrow South Junction, excluding Uxbridge branch but including Chesham branch transferred to Met. & G.C. Joint Committee from April 2nd 1906 until Nationalisation.
11·6 PINNER
10·7 NORTH HARROW
Opened March 22nd 1915
TO UXBRIDGE
16·5 miles from Baker St. Junc.
UXBRIDGE branch opened July 4th 1904 and electrified January 1st 1905.
9·5 HARROW-on-the HILL
Locomotive change point July 19th 1908 to January 4th 1925
Harrow South Junction
Opened March 31st 1901. Delay in opening G.C.R. tracks north of Preston Road Junction caused by late delivery of girder work for bridges.
8·6 NORTHWICK PARK
Opened June 28th 1923
7·6 PRESTON ROAD
Opened as Halt, May 21st 1908
New station opened November 22nd 1931
Preston Road Junction
Removed March 31st 1901
To STANMORE (11·2 miles from Baker St. Junc.)
Opened Dec. 10. 1932, served by Bakerloo Line only from November 20th 1939.
6·7 WEMBLEY PARK
Opened May 12th 1894 Locomotive change point - November 1st 1906 - January 4th 1925
GENERATING STATION
Built by Metropolitan Railway for 1905 electrification
NEASDEN DEPOT
On site of original Metropolitan Railway Works, now main Metropolitan Line depot and largest London Transport running depot.
5·3 NEASDEN
4·8 DOLLIS HILL
Opened October 1st 1909
Served mainly by Bakerloo Line trains from Nov. 20th 1939.
4·0 WILLESDEN GREEN
Locomotive change point for some trains from 1905
Four-tracking of Willesden Green - Kilburn Junc. section delayed by engineering difficulties in widening Kilburn Viaduct
3·3 KILBURN
Kilburn Junction
2·6 WEST HAMPSTEAD
2·2 FINCHLEY ROAD
1·9 SWISS COTTAGE
Metropolitan station closed August 18th 1940
1·4 MARLBOROUGH ROAD
Closed November 19, 1939
0·8 LORD'S
Closed November 19, 1939
Opened as St. John's Wood Railway single track in what is now southbound tunnel. Line doubled for the extension to West Hampstead. St. John's Wood Railway taken over by Metropolitan on January 1st 1883
0·1 BAKER STREET
To PADDINGTON
To FARRINGDON opened Jan. 10th 1863
Baker Street Junction (Mileage datum point)
No through service at Baker Street Junction from March 1869 to January 1907, when a very limited service was re-introduced. Through service between the City and Met. & G.C. line commenced July 1st 1909
To Marylebone - originally Great Central Railway now British Railways (London Midland Region)
Harrow - Rickmansworth September 10, 1961
Baker Street - Uxbridge January 1st 1905 (First trial trip December 13th 1904
May 2, 1948 extra tracks
January 10. 1932
January 4, 1914 - January 11, 1914
Nov. 30, 1913 May 31, 1915
May 25, 1885
August 2, 1880
November 24, 1879
June 30 1879
April 13, 1868
ELECTRIFICATION DATES
FOUR - TRACKING DATES
OPENING DATES
MILEAGE FROM BAKER ST JUNCTION
KEY TO STATIONS
served by all tracks
served by (or to be served by) local tracks only
not normally served by Metropolitan Line trains
closed
Station names are those in current use and not necessarily the original names

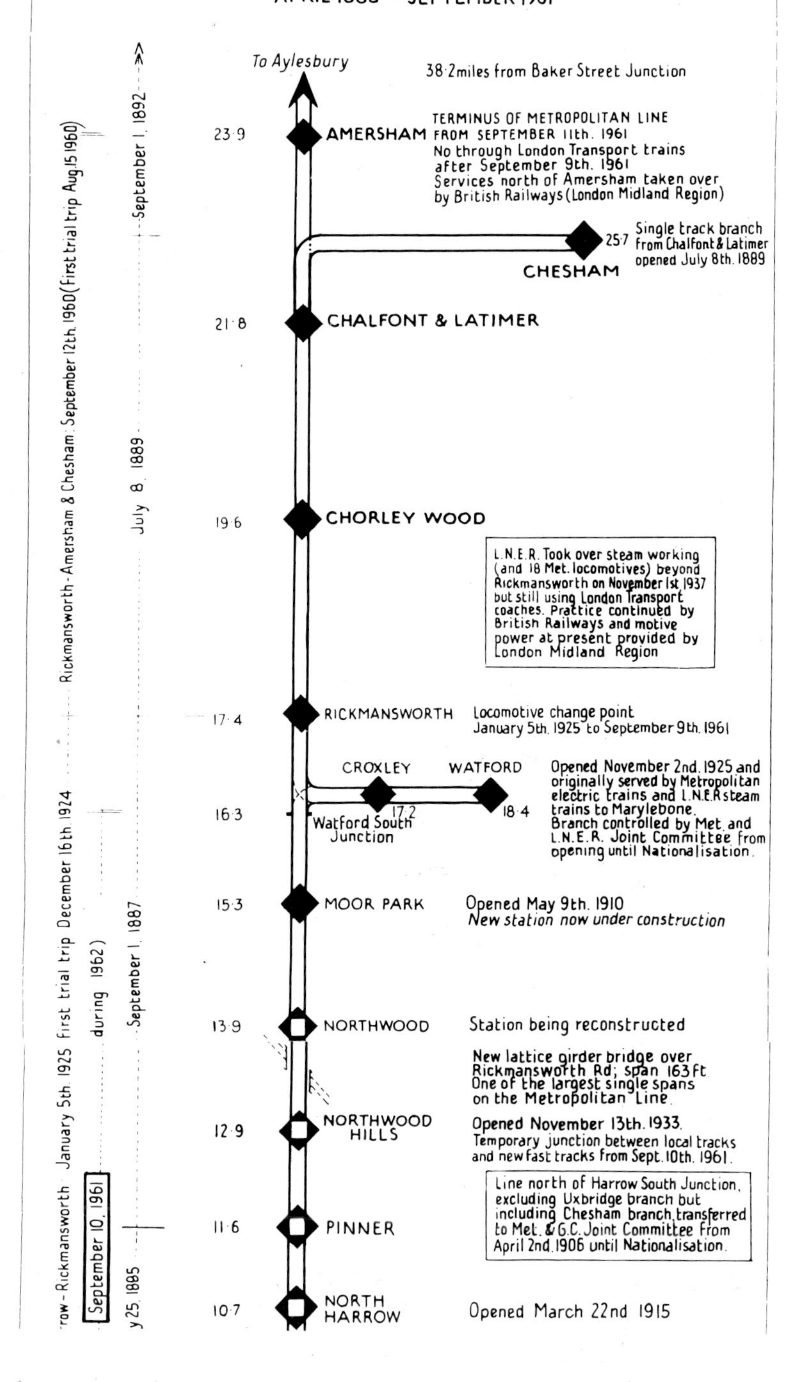

The
METROPOLITAN
BAKER STREET - AMERSHAM
APRIL 1868 - SEPTEMBER 1961
To Aylesbury
38·2 miles from Baker Street Junction
23·9
AMERSHAM
TERMINUS OF METROPOLITAN LINE FROM SEPTEMBER 11th. 1961
No through London Transport trains after September 9th. 1961
Services north of Amersham taken over by British Railways (London Midland Region)
25·7
CHESHAM
Single track branch from Chalfont & Latimer opened July 8th. 1889
21·8
CHALFONT & LATIMER
19·6
CHORLEY WOOD
L.N.E.R. Took over steam working (and 18 Met. locomotives) beyond Rickmansworth on November 1st 1937 but still using London Transport coaches. Practice continued by British Railways and motive power at present provided by London Midland Region
17·4
RICKMANSWORTH
Locomotive change point January 5th. 1925 to September 9th. 1961
CROXLEY
WATFORD
17·2
18·4
16·3
Watford South Junction
Opened November 2nd. 1925 and originally served by Metropolitan electric trains and L.N.E.R. steam trains to Marylebone.
Branch controlled by Met. and L.N.E.R. Joint Committee from opening until Nationalisation.
15·3
MOOR PARK
Opened May 9th. 1910
New station now under construction
13·9
NORTHWOOD
Station being reconstructed
New lattice girder bridge over Rickmansworth Rd; span 163 ft
One of the largest single spans on the Metropolitan Line.
12·9
NORTHWOOD HILLS
Opened November 13th. 1933.
Temporary junction between local tracks and new fast tracks from Sept. 10th. 1961.
11·6
PINNER
Line north of Harrow South Junction, excluding Uxbridge branch but including Chesham branch, transferred to Met. & G.C. Joint Committee from April 2nd. 1906 until Nationalisation.
10·7
NORTH HARROW
Opened March 22nd 1915
row - Rickmansworth January 5th. 1925 First trial trip December 16th. 1924
Rickmansworth - Amersham & Chesham September 12th. 1960 (First trial trip Aug. 15 1960)
September 10, 1961
during 1962)
y 25. 1885
September 1. 1887
July 8. 1889
September 1. 1892

The Victorian ambience of the 'Ladies Only' compartment of the Ashbury coaches with net luggage rack, drop-down window and slam door which closed with a brass lock proudly emblazoned - 'Live in MetroLand'. The Luggage compartment next door was a favourite spot in winter for the crew between trips, as it had extra heating! (*Clive Foxell*)

The C13's were built as class 9K by the GCR and were later fitted with vacuum control gear to enable them to be driven from the end of the far coach. As the war progressed the LNER logo on the tank sides was reduced to just NE, and here 5193 rests alongside the small coaling facilities at Chesham with Fireman, Ken Palmer, alongside. (*Ron White*)

On a cold winter's day 5115 breasts the climb out of the Chess Valley and from this angle the characteristic domed roof of the cab can be seen. In a bad winter the 'Shuttle' would be run through the night to try to keep the track clear of snow, however once the train had to be abandoned near Hodd's Wood and dug out the next day.

The 'through' MET trains from the City were hauled at speed by swaying Bo-Bo electric locos to Rickmansworth where there was a slick changeover to steam traction for the rest of the journey. This was often the lot of tired ex-LNER class N5 0-6-2T's and on the 12th April 1947 no.9257 leaves 'Ricky' heading for Chesham. (*Clive Foxell Collection*)

During the 1940's the Stationmaster was Mr Sidney Taylor, seen here in the centre of a group at Chesham Station. Everyone is neatly turned out and are possibly his colleagues. Mr Taylor started as a clerk on the MET before finally settling at Chesham where he won many prizes for the station gardens before retiring in 1952. (*Michael Hance*)

By this stage often only the loco number was cleaned for identification purposes. A LNER A5 and ex GCR Class 9N 4-6-4T no.9820 with an up MET train from Aylesbury enters Chalfont & Latimer to connect with the 'Shuttle'. (H C Casserley)

The railways were nationalised in 1948 and the ex-LNER engines were re-numbered with a prefix of '6'. On the 16th June 1951, C13 no.67416 has been detached from the 'Shuttle' coaches probably in order to shunt some goods wagons before the next trip, whilst a stationman rests on the running board, waiting to re-couple the set. (A N Davenport)

BR purchased a number of experimental lightweight diesel railbuses in an endeavour to lower running costs on unremunerative branch lines. Such a 3-car set of 4-wheel vehicles from ACV, and powered with 125hp engines, was tried for 2 weeks on the Chesham branch. However they were not a success and had difficulty negotiating the curves. Here in the bay at Chalfont & Latimer on 13th October 1952 the driver is Albert Copperthwaite, who has left his colleagues in a C13 at Chesham as a back up. (*Ron White Collection*)

LT continued to operate a few ex-MET locomotives for maintenance trains and on 22nd May 1955 the ‘Railway World’ magazine organised a tour with 5 Dreadnought coaches hauled by an E class 0-4-4T. Here no. L44 ex-MET no.1 returns from the Chesham leg to go under Bell Lane Bridge approaching Chalfont & Latimer. (*Ron White Collection*)

In July 1951 the daily pick-up freight train waits in Chalfont & Latimer yard to move onto Amersham. No. 69060 was built by Robinson of the GCR, became no.5341 class L3 in the LNER, and ends in BR plain black livery with it’s number on the sides of the bunker. (*P Ransome-Wallis*)

On 16th June 1955 no.67418 cautiously climbs round the bend on the branch near Quill Hall as it approaches an 'arrow' warning sign beside the line, marking maintenance work in progress on the track. Even today, the 'Shuttle' stops to pick up any of the permanent way staff who wants a lift back from a job along the branch. (*Ron White Collection*)

A C13 simmers gently during a formal LT inspection of Chesham Station on the 15th March 1953. The group from left to right are Alex Webb (General Superintendent), Colonel Gordon Maxwell of Ardwell (Operating Manager - Railways), A B Valentine (Chairman, LT Executive) and the Stationmaster, Henry 'John' Hudson with the customary flower in his buttonhole. (*Jean Catherine*)

The entrance to Chesham Station on the 11th August 1955 looks much the same as when it opened and as it does today, except for the price of the tickets on offer. Before the last war a junior member of staff had the job of sweeping the forecourt each day and on Good Friday roping it off in order to formally establish LT ownership. (*LT Museum*)

Thompson's post-war L1 design for the LNER made their debut on the MET in 1948 and here no.67774 on an up train with a Gresley coach behind pulls a rake of mixed stock into Chalfont & Latimer. (*Stephen Gradidge*)

With the 'Shuttle' at Chalfont & Latimer in the background, a LNER-designed class B1 4-6-0 no.61368 pulls away on 11th September 1954 for Aylesbury with a set of Gresley suburban coaches. Like many post-war engines it had a short life, being built in 1950 and scrapped in 1962. (*Stephen Gradidge*)

The driver inspecting C13 no.67418 at Chesham. The hard water supply caused problems with build-up of scale in the boiler and many types of chemical treatment were tried. However, several members of the footplate staff have mentioned that this did not seem to affect the fish that lived in the side tanks! This is not quite as far-fetched as it might seem as a number of water towers along the line were fed from un-filtered streams. (*Ron White*)

The classic picture of the 'Shuttle' with no.67416 crossing the original two-span bridge over the River Chess at The Moor. Alas, no longer would one be able to stroll hand-in-hand, without a care, down the middle of that road without danger of being runover. The photo was taken by Alan Willmott of Windjammer Films, who also shot a charming 16mm film of the steam operation of the Chesham Branch, which is now incorporated in a video.

In 1956 it was still possible to travel from Chesham to Harrow on the Hill or Aylesbury and catch an express train - including a restaurant car - to the north. Six trains per day went to destinations such as Sheffield and Manchester, and here the up 16.50 ex-Marylebone 'South Yorkshireman' bound for Bradford passes Chorleywood Common headed by ex-LNER B1 4-6-0 no.61299. (*Stephen Gradidge*)

On the 13th October 1956 an A3 4-6-2 no.60111 "Enterprise" with a high-sided tender leans into the curve at Chorleywood with the morning up 'Master Cutler' from Sheffield which took about 3½ hours for the journey to Marylebone. A3's were withdrawn from the GC route within the year. (*Stephen Gradidge*)

In 1957 goods still generated a considerable amount of traffic along the Extension. On the 23rd March an ex-LNER K3 class 2-6-0 no.61866 pulls an up fitted-freight past the yard at Chalfont & Latimer. (*Stephen Gradidge*)

In 1957 responsibility passed to the Midland Region (ex-LMS) and this inevitably brought changes in motive power. Briefly, an ex LMS Fowler 2-6-4T no.42358 was loaned from the Kentish Town Shed to haul the 'through' Chesham train. This rare picture was taken in poor light, as the evening train was about to leave Chesham. (*Ron White Collection*)

An ex-LMS tank on a mainline down train is in the background whilst the connecting 'Shuttle' with Neasden-based no.67420 waits in the Chalfont & Latimer bay platform. (*Ron White Collection*)

Civil engineering work re-started in 1959 on electrifying the line beyond Rickmansworth and by January 1960 a new bay was being constructed at Chesham. This involved excavating the gardens, lengthening the platform for the new LT 8-car electric sets and removing the watercrane that was replaced by an ex-GWR water tower. (*LT Museum*)

The scene at Chalfont & Latimer with the new conductor rails in place and an ex-LMS 2-6-4T no.42178 pulling into the up platform. One dark night the stopping train overshot this platform and a passenger fell out, however luckily he went head-first into a pile of rubbish that the staff had dumped at this point and he emerged without injury. (*NMR*)

Electrification at Chalfont & Latimer involved lengthening the down platform and installing an extra crossing over to the branch in order to accommodate the new longer LT stock.. Towards the end of the steam era on 11.9.1960 with a clean ex-works Fairburn 4MT 2-6-4T no.42066 heads a MET train from Aylesbury. (*Stephen Gradidge*)

A little later a BR standard Class 5 4-6-0 no.73159 passes through Chalfont & Latimer with an up Nottingham - Marylebone express. The new colour-light signals are now in place. (*Stephen Gradidge*)

The electrification of the branch involved a new signalling system and here at Chesham during the summer of 1960 John Hudson, the Stationmaster who was shortly to retire, looks down from the window of the signalbox onto a contractor who is re-wiring a terminal cabinet. (*Jean Catherine*)

The interior of the Chesham signalbox, which was of the standardised MET design, with signalman Fred Cooper holding the no.3 starter lever covered with the traditional yellow duster to preserve the high degree of polish on the handle. (*Fred Cooper*)

On the 21st August 1960 with the new bay, conductor rails and water tower in place, most of the conversion work at Chesham had been completed. One of the ex-LMS Ivatt 2-6-2T engines no.41284 that took over from the old C13's stands ready to depart with the 'Shuttle'. *(R C Riley)*

The first trial of running electric stock on the Chesham branch took place on 15th August 1960. Existing MET stock had to be used due to delays in the completion of the new multiple electric trains. Thus the 6-car set of 'T'stock stands at the original platform, whilst engine no.41284 waits with the 'Shuttle' in the bay for the arrival of the daily steam-hauled pick-up goods train. *(LT Museum)*

Veteran MET Bo-Bo electric locomotives were also pressed into service for the 'through' Amersham and Chesham trains. This is a test run with no.7 'Edmund Burke' leaving the branch by the original crossover at Chalfont & Latimer but later one of this class was timed at over 60 mph downhill into Chesham. (*Brian Stephenson*)

A 3-car T set in MTM configuration replaced the steam 'Shuttle' until the overdue new A60 stock were delivered. During this period a somewhat enthusiastic motorman entered Chalfont and Latimer station rather quickly and demolished the buffers at the end of the bay platform. Henceforth he was always known as 'Flyer'. (*Jean Catherine Collection*)

The last scheduled steam passenger train ran on the branch on 12th September 1960 with all the usual ceremonies. A suitably wreathed no.41284 is having its sidetanks filled from the ex-GW water tower. (*Ron White*)

At the end of the trip no.41284 arrives at Chalfont & Latimer with its three Ashbury coaches full of enthusiasts and local people paying farewells. As the LT Magazine commented "the sound of the engine puffing energetically up the gradient with its sixty year-old coaches had become part of the life for residents in the area. Now the electric trains have come and the hills and valleys are strangely silent". (*Stephen Gradidge*)

The 'Shuttle' on the return trip to Chesham being driven from the end trailer compartment and photographed from Raans Bridge. In the background the line curves round into Chalfont where, when the 'Shuttle' raced the mainline train, cinders from the engine sometimes set fire to Boughton's fields. (*Ray East*)

The delivery of the 'aluminium' A60 electric stock was completed in 1962 and this photo shows Ernie Woodstock, now promoted to Stationmaster in charge of the local group of stations, talking to a guard of one of the new trains. Later the MET moved to 'one person' operation and such guards disappeared. (*Phyllis Woodstock*)

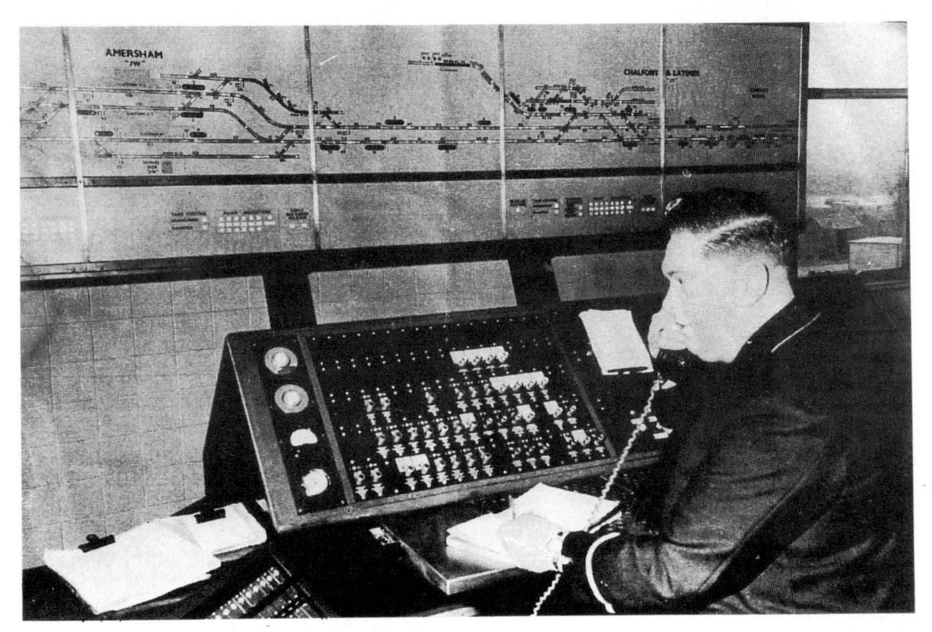

New signalling arrangements for the branch were brought into operation in 1962 with the concentration of control at the box at Amersham. Here Don Grant supervises the console and in the background the diagram shows that the sidings at Amersham and Chalfont are still in use whilst those at Chesham have been removed from the panel. (*LT Magazine*)

Diesels began to replace steam in 1961 and on 3rd August an up stopping train approaches the footbridge north of Chalfont & Latimer, with the Chesham branch in the background. The train is double-headed by two grimy B1 4-6-0's, 61136 & 61028. Unlikely to require such an array of motive power, one engine was probably being worked back 'light' to Neasden Shed. The last scheduled steam express ran in 1966. (*Stephen Gradidge*)

Even at the end to the parcels service Chesham was handling some 65,000 items a year. Christmas was the busiest time and a nostalgic array of parcels is being sorted in December 1966. Foreman Kenny Neale, bending down and Billy Butterfield (ticket collector) at the rear are checking details with Bob Bignall (parcels clerk). *(Bob Bignall)*

The office went first when the goods shed at Chesham was demolished to make room for a car park. So went all the memories of the piles of wicker baskets for watercress, named 'flats' (28lb) and 'chips' (7-10lb), and the smelly fish crates awaiting reuse. Mysteriously, the occasional kipper had found its way to be a stationman's breakfast. *(Ray East)*

The electrified branch also has its share of incidents. Apparently a van being loaded with hay from a field near the Pioneer Hall at Chesham Bois ran away and went down the embankment in front of an oncoming evening Chesham-bound 'Shuttle'. Trains were severely delayed but fortunately nobody was injured. (*Ron White Collection*)

A 1983 view from the cab of the 'Shuttle' as the train crossed the old Moor Bridge. The LT Magazine described it: "the line climbs steadily into the beautiful, wooded Chiltern Hills - full of twists and turns the only tunnel is a natural one - tall trees lining a steep cutting have climbed and overlapped to form a green roof over the tracks". (*Clive Foxell*)

The problem of 'leaves on the line' increased in recent years and many strange techniques have been tried for removing them. In November 1984 this road-rail mounted blower was driven along the track from Chalfont car park. Needless to say it did not work and in the end resort had to be made to the traditional solution of cutting back the undergrowth.

Due to lack of funds to replace the weakened bridges at Chesham, LT proposed to again terminate the branch at The Moor. Fortunately at the eleventh hour support came from the GLC Residuary Body. The new single-span bridges were erected alongside the old and this changeover at Waterside took place on 24th March 1986. (*Clive Foxell*)

The Centenary of the branch in July 1989 was celebrated in fine style with a steam service between Chesham and Watford operated by the newly restored MET E class tank loco no.1 from Quainton Road. The down train is here at Chalfont & Latimer waiting to have access to the branchline with the LT 'Shuttle' in the background. (*Clive Foxell*)

Following the success of the Centenary specials a number of 'Steam on the MET' events have been held on the Extension over recent years. This has attracted other visitors to the Chesham branch including various LUL stock, such as this C69/77 Circle Line 4-car set, which replaced the usual A60 'Shuttle' on the 6th May 1996. (*Clive Foxell*)

The Extension has always seen a good variety of visiting motive power, probably reaching a high spot during the BR locomotive trials of June 1948 when a LMS Class 5 no.45253, a GW Hall no.6990 and a SR West Country Class 'Bude' - giving a particularly rousing performance - thundered through Chalfont & Latimer. Bringing back memories of this time, one of the visiting engines during the May 1996 'Steam on the MET' was the GW Mogul 7325, here seen on a rainy day with an down train at Chalfont. (*Ron Potter*)

Various LUL Service trains involved in track maintenance traverse the Chesham Branch from time to time. This 2-car set of 1938 Bakerloo Line stock, painted bright yellow, was spraying weed-killer during a visit in April 1998. In heavy rain, the rear of the train is passing under the footbridge at the 'Backs' on the approach to Chesham. (*Clive Foxell*)

The major refurbishment of the A60 stock started in 1993 however, just as in the old MET and GCR times, their riding qualities leave much to be desired in comparison with the mainline Turbo-Diesels of Chiltern Railways. In the autumn of 1997 a refurbished train arrives in Chesham set in its prize-winning floral display. It remains the furthermost outpost of LT and the greatest distance from another LT station. (*Clive Foxell*)

For the 'Steam on the MET' event in 1998 the recently restored ex-LNER Thompson designed B1class 4-6-0 engine no.1264 in apple green livery heads a rake of LUL maroon coaches through Chalfont & Latimer. The magnificent sight of this loco working hard on the climb through the Chilterns turns the clock back almost 40 years. (*Clive Foxell*)